A Dictionary of HOPTANGLISH

(a language knot to mention)

DAVID CATCHPOOLE

Zafferona Press

Published by Zafferona Press

First Edition
ISBN-13: 978-0995394308
1. Language 2. Humour 3. Fantasy
Cover design by Ana Grigoriu

This book is dedicated to the voiceless.

Contents

Acknowledgements

This book would not have been possible without an unwavering
belief in the impossible.

Abbreviations

adj.	adjective
adv.	adverb
int.	interjection
n.	noun
nm.	mass noun
pl. n.	plural noun
pro.	pronoun
vt.	verb, transitive
vi.	verb, intransitive
vt./i.	verb, transitive or intransitive
Ar.	Arabic
Au.	Australian
Br.	British
Du.	Dutch
Fr.	French
Ge.	German
Gr.	Greek
Gu.	Gullah
Hp.	Hoptanglish
It.	Italian
J.	Japanese
L.	Latin
ON.	Old Norse
R.	Russian
Sc.	Scottish
Sp.	Spanish
US	United States
inf.	informal
obs.	obsolete

Introduction

Like many other languages, Hoptanglish began as a dialect, emerging gradually from English over many generations, until its speakers suddenly realized what they just said. They had stumbled upon an awareness that their way of communicating was distinct to their little neighbourhood, and that it wasn't quite English anymore. Language, therefore, is more than a vocabulary or grammar; it is a consciousness of connection to other speakers. It is a truly amazing tool, and as it develops it allows more sophisticated methods for people to make themselves misunderstood. It is the role of dictionary-makers to record this hubbub in its entirety, because if they focused only on the utterances that actually made sense, they'd be out of a job.

Hoptanglish is spoken in the land of Hoptanglia. A traveller to such a distant, foreign place would expect to find many differences, and such differences do indeed abound there, such as electric monkeys. But perhaps more unexpected are the similarities, such as the non-electric monkeys that you and I are used to. (Some shrewd hotel operators, when welcoming a foreign guest, fill the bathroom with these non-electric monkeys to reduce the culture shock.) Likewise, when you speak with the natives you will recognise many English words. The language exists as a continuum, with a "thinner", more English variety in some regions and a "thicker", more Hoptanglish variety in other regions. This makes it ideal for anyone wanting to learn the language. It is very easy to dip your toe in the shallow end; to pepper your normal speech with one or two Hoptanglish words. After that, you can delve into the thicker, richer depths to your heart's content and your soul's confusiasm.

Don't just speak your mind.

Sing your imagination!

A

addle-essence *(nm.)*
the state of being a teenager with an identity crisis.

airball *(n.)*
a bubble that has been peeled.

airobe *(n.)*
a microscopic organism that likes to keep fit by floating about in the air for at least fifteen minutes every day.
[a blend of *air* + *microbe*.]

airpork *(n.)*
a flying pig.

antinoun *(n.)*
a pronoun's opposite, such as "he" in relation to "she", or "you" in relation to "me".

aptable *(adj.)*
capable of being suitable.

aukward *(adv.)*
towards an auk.

avocadive *(adj.)*
reminiscent of the taste, smell or texture of avocados.
[a blend of *avocado* + *evocative*.]

awlwright *(n.)*
a craftsman who fashions awls.

awmirrawmemawrial *(n.)*
an ominous gravestone that bears a reference to the person looking at it, such as their name or image.
[a blend of *awe* + *mirror* + *memorial*.]

B

baptoid *(n.)*
any partially terrestrialized creature that still has to dip its head under water to think properly.
[from Gr. *baptizein* 'immerse' + *-oid*.]

barkduckerish *(adj.)*
dodging falling branches or trees.

batmatter *(n.)*
a craze.
[from inf. *bats* 'mad' + *matter*.]

bazoobabushka *(n.)*
an old lady with a rocket launcher.
[a blend of *bazooka* + Ru. *babushka* 'grandmother'.]

beatburner *(n.)*
an appliance that syncs the flicker of a candle's flame to the rhythm of the music being played.

beerdrum *(n.)*
a keg.

befundle *(vt.)*
to amuse and confuse.
[a blend of *befuddle* + *fun*.]

bellicherent *(adj.)*
burping aggressively.
[a blend of *belch* +
belligerent.]

bespaggle *(vt.)*
to drench in pasta.
[from *be-* + *spaghetti* +
-le.]

betterbother *(n.)*
a more suitable
inconvenience.

beway *(n.)*
a mode of existence.

bibliokado *(n.)*
a gatefold or other portal in
a book through which you
can step into a different
book.
[from *biblio-* + J. *kado*
'gate'.]

bifurgrey *(n.)*
a brain that splits in two as
soon as it gets to the point.
[a blend of *bifurcate* +
grey.]

blammage *(nm.)*
food which has been spilt,
burnt, smashed, etc.
[a blend of *blancmange* +
damage.]

blobombrill *(n.)*
a letter that's been
smudged by rain.
[a blend of *blob* + Gr.

ombros 'rain' + *bill*.]

bloss *(n.)*
a bonsai plant.
[a curtail of *blossom*.]

blunderbustle *(nm.)*
clumsy busyness.

bogglebogged *(adj.)*
encumbered by
conundrums.

bonbonjuka *(int.)*
hello.
[a blend of *bonbon* + Gu.
juke 'disorderly' + Fr.
bonjour 'hello'.]

bonster *(n.)*
a friend.
[a blend of Fr. *bon* 'good' +
monster.]

bonzaquince *(n.)*
a very good outcome.
[a blend of Au. inf. *bonzer*
'excellent' + *consequence* +
quince.]

bootfall *(nm.)*
barefoot football.

bovoid *(n.)*
a robot that resembles a
cow.
[a blend of *bovine* +
android.]

bragend *(n.)*
a criminal who gets caught
by boasting about their
crime.
[a blend of *brag* +
brigand.]

breakermaker *(n.)*
a controversial sculptor who makes waves by scooping away the water around them.

breverie *(n.)*
a momentary daydream.
[a blend of *brevity* + *reverie*.]

bunglewright *(n.)*
a professional maker of mistakes.

bussoon *(n.)*
a bus horn.
[a blend of *bus* + *bassoon*.]

butterdial *(n.)*
a melting clock.

buzmo *(n.)*
a biomechanical device powered by bees.
[a blend of *buzz* + *gizmo*.]

buzzling *(n.)*
a young bee.

bysket *(n.)*
a basket attached to a bike.
[a blend of *bicycle* + *basket*.]

C

canaryberry *(n.)*
a gooseberry that has been genetically modified to taste like a canary.

cardinella *(n.)*
a female cardinal.

caroon *(vt./i.)*
to drive and sing recklessly.
[a blend of *careen* + *croon*.]

cascabraid *(n.)*
1. two or more entwined waterfalls.
2. a partner dance.
[a blend of *cascade* + *braid*.]

catapoultry *(pl. n.)*
projectile fowls.
[a blend of *catapult* + *poultry*.]

causewell *(n.)*
a catalyst of good fortune.

checkerbockers *(nm.)*
sexual strategy.
[a blend of *checkers* + *knickerbockers*.]

cheekful *(n.)*
half a mouthful.

chookaburra *(n.)*
a cross between a chicken and a kookaburra.
[a blend of Au. inf. *chook* 'chicken' + *kookaburra*.]

choreostume *(nm.)*
the combination or interaction of dance and fashion.
[a blend of Gr. *khoreia* 'dancing' + *costume*.]

chroscent *(n.)*
1. a clock that is partly in

3

darkness, and so appears as a crescent.
2. a window of opportunity.
[a blend of Gr. *khronos* 'time' + *crescent*.]

clamburger *(n.)*
a greedy clam with several layers of food stuffed between its jaws, sometimes served as a dish.

clicotine *(nm.)*
an addictive substance that gives you a little buzz whenever you click on something.
[a blend of *click* + *nicotine*.]

clip-clop-flip-flop *(n.)*
a casual horseshoe.

clogbond *(n.)*
a relationship that's going nowhere.

commadashery *(nm.)*
excessive punctuation.

commanucate *(vt./i.)*
to talk with your hands.
[a blend of *communicate* + L. *manus* 'hand'.]

confusiastic *(adj.)*
eagerly bewildered.
[a blend of *confused* + *enthusiastic*.]

contrapinquity *(nm.)*
irrelevance.
[from *contra-* + *propinquity*.]

cornshot *(adj.)*
damaged by an eavesdropper.
[from *corn*, in reference to its ears + *shot*.]

cracklewax *(nm.)*
fizzy jam.

cramblather *(vt./i.)*
to talk with your mouth full.

crayslaw *(n.)*
a salad inhabited by seafood.
[a blend of *crayfish* + Du. *slaw* 'salad'.]

curlicurial *(adj.)*
twirly and capricious.
[a blend of *curlicue* + *mercurial*.]

curridge *(nm.)*
curried porridge, often eaten to induce bravery.

curtail *(n.)*
a word formed by removing letters from the end of another word.

custopo *(n.)*
a tangled octopus.
[a jufflenym of *octopus*.]

𝒟

dachshundite *(n.)*
a fossil of a dachshund.
[from *dachshund* + *-ite*.]

dawnish *(adj.)*
beginning to teach.

deckle *(vt./i.)*
to write.
[derivation uncertain;
probably from *declare*.]

deckleduff *(nm.)*
loose notes; disorganized
scribbles.
[from Hp. *deckle* + Sc. *duff*
'vegetable matter decaying
on the ground beneath
trees'.]

decoderm *(nm.)*
skin used as a canvas.
[a blend of *decoration* +
Gr. *derma* 'skin'.]

deligoat *(n.)*
a pack animal used as a
shopping trolley.

delvish *(adj.)*
very curious.

deostricant *(n.)*
a body spray that repels
ostriches.

depressionism *(nm.)*
a sluggish art movement
that vainly seeks to capture
the effects that light
doesn't seem to have
anymore.

dibiliboon *(n.)*
a disability used as an
advantage.
[a blend of *debilitate* +
boon.]

dilapidalia *(pl. n.)*
fragments of remnants.
[from *dilapidate* + -*alia*.]

diprot *(nm.)*
water damage.

discapsulate *(vi.)*
to spill your brevity all
over the place.
[from *dis-* + *capsule* +
-*ate*.]

disfigraphy *(nm.)*
mangled handwriting.
[from *disfigure* +
-*graphy*.]

disorienteering *(nm.)*
the sport of getting lost.
[a blend of *disorientate* +
orienteering.]

distraction span *(n.)*
the amount of time that you
can stay distracted.

dodecadiesel *(n.)*
a twelve-wheeled truck.
[from *dodeca-* + *diesel*.]

doortime *(n.)*
the time at which is
appropriate to arrive or
leave.

downchairs *(adv.)*
off a chair and onto the
floor.

downrising *(n.)*
a U-turn in an uprising.

downtrain *(adv.)*
towards the front of a train.

drenchcoat *(n.)*

a sabotaged raincoat.

dropolodot *(n.)*
someone who misses the whole point.
[a blend of *drop* + Hp. *holodot*.]

dropstops *(pl. n.)*
tiny plugs for leaky tear ducts.

dropzap *(n.)*
a great idea you have just as you're falling asleep.

dublop *(n.)*
a word formed by removing letters from the beginning and ending of another word.
[a blend of *double* + *lop*.]

duckness *(nm.)*
the state of being a duck.

duecumbered *(adj.)*
hampered by deadlines.
[from *due* + *cumbered*.]

dukebox *(n.)*
a glove with a plectrum on the end of each finger.
[a blend of inf. *duke* 'fist' + *jukebox*.]

dwelve *(vi.)*
to live (or writhe) in a state of perpetual research.
[a blend of *dwell* + *delve*.]

dwindlebooth *(n.)*
a shrinking elevator.

e

echovex *(vt.)*
to annoy someone by repeating everything they say.

eeb *(n.)*
a bee that can fly backwards.
[a reversal of *bee*.]

elasupposatix *(nm.)*
the stretchy property of imaginations.
[a blend of *elastic* + *suppose* + a fanciful suffix.]

elboword *(n.)*
a blend word in which the last letter of the first word is used as the first letter of the last word, such as sudduration from sud and duration, or junketackler from junket and tackler.
[an elboword of *elbow* + *word*.]

ergle *(vt./i.)*
to steal someone's job.
[a blend of Gr. *ergon* 'work' + *burgle*.]

erosperil *(nm.)*
danger as an aphrodisiac.

errorverity *(nm.)*
reality that is incorrectly displayed.

eurigma *(int.)*

an exclamation of triumph for having reached a higher state of confusion.
[a blend of *eureka* + *enigma*.]

everberry *(n.)*
a fruit that never rots.

evolition *(n.)*
the gradual development of free will over many generations by natural selection and personal choice.
[a blend of *evolution* + *volition*.]

excuisitelicacy *(n.)*
a food of the finest, most excuisitive quality.
[a blend of Hp. *excuisitive* + *delicacy*.]

excuisitive *(adj.)*
curiously delicious.
[a blend of *exquisite* + *cuisine* + *inquisitive*.]

exhilarant *(nm.)*
rollercoaster fuel.

expectacular *(adj.)*
formerly amazing and brilliant, but now just overexposed, passé or predictable.

F

faithlift *(n.)*
a spiritual renovation.

fascofied *(adj.)*
proud of being a disappointment.
[a blend of *fiasco* + *satisfied*.]

featherside *(adv., adj.)*
next to a bird.

febricate *(vt./i.)*
to engage in artistic creation while in a state of sickness.
[a blend of L. *febris* 'fever' + *fabricate*.]

fedbellow *(n.)*
a belch.

feisterplaster *(nm.)*
living clay.
[from *feisty* + *plaster*.]

ferretocracy *(n.)*
government by ferrets.

filliphilia *(nm.)*
love of horses.
[from *filly* + *-philia*.]

finchflinch *(vt./i.)*
to imitate the body language of birds.

fingerpit *(n.)*
the place between two fingers at their base.

flairspurn *(nm.)*
disdain for greatness.

flamesplitter *(n.)*
a massive migraine in the sun.

flaxenfeld *(nm.)*
parchment or paper that is

bought, sold, measured and used as real estate.
[from *flaxen* 'pale yellow' + Ge. *Feld* 'field'.]

fledgucate *(vt.)*
to teach how to fly.
[a blend of *fledge* + *educate*.]

flipperflapper *(n.)*
a wing adapted for swimming.

floraglorify *(vt./i.)*
to worship plants.

flumbuxuriate *(vi.)*
to wallow.
[a blend of *flump* + *luxuriate*.]

flupple *(vt./i.)*
to turn inside out.
[derivation uncertain; probably from *flip*.]

flutterswipe *(n.)*
someone who is annoying but defenceless.

fogmash *(n.)*
a flying steamroller.

fooligan *(n.)*
a stupid troublemaker.
[a blend of *fool* + *hooligan*.]

footkerchief *(n.)*
a triangular piece of fabric used to wipe mud, treacle, etc. from between the toes.

forboidence *(nm.)*
the prohibition of

prophesy.
[a blend of *forebode* 'to anticipate' + *forbiddance*.]

fordwater *(n.)*
a place where stagnation is impossible, thanks to regular crossovers.

foreforce *(nm.)*
careful and prudent action, especially when it is done to avoid hasty or reckless thought.

fornoolishing *(adj.)*
nutritiously injudicious.
[a blend of *foolish* + *nourishing*.]

fountaineering *(nm.)*
the extreme sport of climbing fountains.

fragitarian *(adj.)*
feeding on delicacies.

frecklebox *(n.)*
a photo album.

freeee *(n.)*
someone who is freed.
[from *free* + *-ee*.]

frenetics *(pl. n.)*
fevered speech.
[a blend of *frenetic* + *phonetics*.]

frolibog *(vt./i.)*
to paralyse the spirit of play with analysis.
[a blend of *frolic* + *bog*.]

frustacitosis *(nm.)*
a strong desire and inability

to speak.
[a blend of *frustration* + L.
tacitus 'silent' + *-osis*.]

fulcrumb *(n.)*
either half of a diagonally
cut sandwich; a tasty
triangle on which to
balance a diet.
[a tiakler of *fulcrum* +
crumb.]

fumblejack *(n.)*
an apprentice
bunglewright.

funbud *(n.)*
a sense organ that detects
humour.

furlap *(n.)*
a skywinder kept as a pet.
[an elboword of *furl* + *lap*.]

fussmucker *(n.)*
an associate of an
important person.
[from *fuss* + Br. inf.
mucker 'a companion'.]

Q

qualmistice *(n.)*
an uneasy truce.
[a blend of *qualm* +
armistice.]

quarter-hearted *(adj.)*
partially half-hearted.

quespithork *(n.)*
a riddle.
[derivation uncertain;

possibly something to do
with *question, bethink* or
fork.]

quigh *(n.)*
the urge to find the
meaning of life.
[a blend of *question* +
why.]

quineslide *(n.)*
an ice skate worn by horses
in glissage.
[from *equine* + *slide*.]

quink *(nm.)*
living ink.
[a blend of *quick* + *ink*.]

quiplomatic *(adj.)*
managing political affairs
with heartening repartee.
[a blend of *quip* +
diplomatic.]

quiverquill *(n.)*
a shivering porcupine.

quyllabus *(n.)*
a person's writing
vocabulary.
[a blend of *quill* +
syllabus.]

H

haafter *(nm.)*
the sea's laughter.
[a blend of ON *haaf* 'ocean'
+ *laughter*.]

halebale *(nm.)*
suffering which makes you

stronger or healthier.

halover *(n.)*
a saltwater waterfall.
[from *halo-* + *over*.]

handlesome *(adj.)*
dealing well.

hawkus porkus *(n.)*
a pig that flies on a
broomstick; a magical
airpork.
[a blend of *hawk* + *pork* +
hocus-pocus.]

hayrock *(nm.)*
country music.

heartbake *(nm.)*
love.

heftagruntumphous *(adj.)*
struggling to laugh.
[a blend of *heft* + *grunt* +
oomph + *-ous*.]

hogwire *(n.)*
a virus that can jump from
pigs to computers.

holodot *(n.)*
the whole point.
[a blend of Gr. *holos*
'whole' + *dot*.]

hoop-cha *(int.)*
an expression of cheeky
jubilation.
[derivation uncertain;
perhaps related to *houp-la*.]

horrorlarious *(adj.)*
shocking, disgusting and
amusing.
[a blend of *horror* +

hilarious.]

hovergraft *(n.)*
an ambulance helicopter.

hufpus *(n.)*
a thief with poor
commitment.
[a blend of *half* + *purse*.]

huglet *(n.)*
a small hug using only the
hands.

hullery *(n.)*
a shipyard.

hybird *(n.)*
a hybrid of two birds, such
as a gooster, chookaburra
or gabudgerilah.
[a blend of *hybrid* + *bird*.]

I

icelead *(nm.)*
lethargy that turns into
paralysis.

icomiconoclast *(n.)*
a humorous heretic.
[a blend of *iconoclast* +
comic.]

igsaw *(n.)*
a jigsaw with a piece
missing.
[a nosetrim of *jigsaw*.]

impeculiar *(adj.)*
perfectly normal,
especially in a sudden or
unexpected way.

[from *im-* + *peculiar*.]

impstitute *(n.)*
a research laboratory where
practical jokes are
developed.
[a blend of *imp* + *institute*.]

incidensity *(nm.)*
the degree to which you
experience something.
[a blend of *incident* +
density.]

infitinerinity *(nm.)*
endless travel.
[a blend of *infinity* + L.
itinerari 'travel'.]

intellectricity *(nm.)*
electric thought.
[a blend of *intellect* +
electricity.]

intermistern *(n.)*
an endless wait for an
inevitable sneeze.
[a blend of *interminable* +
L. *sternuere* 'to sneeze'.]

inth *(nm.)*
the state of being in.

irisphere *(n.)*
a state of mind which is
particularly conducive to
appreciation.
[from Gr. *iris* 'rainbow' +
-sphere.]

irklet *(n.)*
a minor concern.
[from *irk* + *-let*.]

irkule *(n.)*
a gnat.

[from *irk* + *-ule*.]

irrectify *(vt.)*
to accidentally correct a
correctly spelled word or a
fact into a mistake.
[from *ir-* + *rectify*.]

iwrwriggular *(adj.)*
calm.
[from *ir-* + Hp. *wriggular*.]

J

jaloopy *(n.)*
a ramshackle rollercoaster.
[a blend of *jalopy* + *loop*.]

jarkle *(vi.)*
to walk like a seal.
[from obs. *jark* 'seal' + *-le*.]

jawbrained *(adj.)*
obsessed with eating.

jotterfodder *(nm.)*
food in the form of written
words.

jowling *(nm.)*
contemplation.
[from *jowl* + *-ing*.]

jufflenym *(n.)*
a neologism formed as an
anagram.
[from Sc. obs. *juffle* 'to
shuffle' + *-onym*.]

jugboat *(n.)*
a ship with a tall, round
hull.

juggelknot *(n.)*

a pattern woven with skweavers.
[from *juggle* + *knot*.]

junglefuzz *(n.)*
a wild, woolly sheep tousled to distraction.

junketackler *(n.)*
a creature that feeds on picnics.
[an elboword of *junket* + *tackler*.]

jupiterberry *(n.)*
a watermelon.

К

kaustral *(adj.)*
1. burnt on the underside.
2. secretly offended.
[a blend of Gr. *kaustos* 'burnt' + L. *australis* 'southern'.]

kischief *(nm.)*
romantic shenanigans.
[a blend of *kiss* + *mischief*.]

knoppet *(n.)*
a little walking stick used by elderly insects.
[from *knop* 'knob', which is typically featured atop one + *-et*.]

knotwhat *(n.)*
a problem.

kruggle *(n.)*
the collective term for a group of collectors.

[derivation unknown.]

kungfoolery *(nm.)*
martial arts combined with slapstick comedy.
[a blend of *kung fu* + *tomfoolery*.]

Ⅼ

lachrylockage *(n.)*
the quarantining of sadness.
[from L. *lacrima* 'tear' + *lock* + *-age*.]

lackless *(adj.)*
deficient in wants.

lalaborate *(vi.)*
to conduct linguistic experiments.
[a blend of Gr. *lalia* 'speech' + *laboratory* + *-ate*.]

lampsand *(nm.)*
pulverized rice that is fried over an oil lamp and served with a good book.

landguessing *(nm.)*
the pastime of predicting where the ground will be when you've completed your somersault.

larkitecture *(nm.)*
the design of practical jokes.
[a blend of *lark* + *architecture*.]

larriparrokin *(n.)*
a boisterous, uncouth parrot.
[a blend of *larrikin* + *parrot*.]

lather-brained *(adj.)*
fanciful and excitable.

lendthrift *(n.)*
someone who loans recklessly.

leverbeast *(n.)*
a feral robot.

lingustics *(pl. n.)*
the interaction between language and taste. → the study thereof.
[from L. *lingua* 'language' + L. *gustus* 'taste' + -*ics*.]

locust-lily *(n.)*
a beautiful, carnivorous plant with a taste for grasshoppers.

lucidrous *(adj.)*
clearly absurd.
[a blend of *lucid* + *ludicrous*.]

ludicurious *(adj.)*
intrigued by comical incongruities.
[a blend of *ludicrous* + *curious*.]

luniversity *(n.)*
a wobbly college with collapsing faculties that offer dippy diplomas.
[a blend of *lunacy* + *university*.]

M

mailjunk *(n.)*
a sailing letterbox.

malflourished *(adj.)*
deprived of calligraphy.

manywhere *(adv., adj.)*
in or to lots of places.

massarduous *(adj.)*
hard to knead.
[a blend of *massage* + *arduous*.]

meandereaning *(nm.)*
meaning without purpose.
[a blend of *meander* + *meaning*.]

metalgia *(nm.)*
pain caused by metamorphosis.
[from *meta-* + -*algia*.]

millaville *(n.)*
a small town built around a mill.
[from *mill* + Fr. *ville* 'town'.]

millistratisemanticity *(nm.)*
the condition of having many layers of meaning.
[from L. *mille* 'thousand' + *strata* + *semantic* + -*ity*.]

millwasp *(n.)*
a wind-powered helicopter.

miscellanimus *(n.)*
a cocktail.
[a blend of *miscellaneous* +

L. *animus* 'spirit'.]

moultry *(pl. n.)*
any animals or plants that
moult, especially as viewed
and valued by the second-
hand clothing industry.

mountain ant *(n.)*
an extremely ferocious and
uncompromising ant that
lives up in the mountains,
paralyzing and
disembowelling campers,
entomologists, etc. with its
wild exaggeration.

mousepoint *(nm.)*
(in the phrase **at
mousepoint**) hovered over
by a mouse pointer; about
to be clicked on.

muckdush *(n.)*
a pie containing duck meat
and mushrooms.
[a blend of *mushroom +
duck*.]

mudcurdling *(nm.)*
the industrial process of
teasing the dirt out of mud
to produce water.

mugfroth *(nm.)*
facial expressiveness.
[from inf. *mug* 'face' +
froth.]

multiprodular *(adj.)*
having many horns.

murksman *(n.)*
a fuzzy logician.

mushture *(nm.)*

evaporated mud.
[a blend of *mush +
moisture*.]

musterhood *(n.)*
the group of people present
at a meeting.

muzma *(nm.)*
a single fabric consisting of
space, time and thought.
[a blend of *muse +
plasma*.]

Ŋ

nanaluna *(n.)*
a crescent moon.
[from *banana* + L. *luna*
'moon'.]

nanodecade *(n.)*
a decade that rushes past
without you even noticing.

naptally *(vt./i.)*
to count the sleeps to go
before a certain day.

nephonate *(vi.)*
to swim in a cloud.
[from Gr. *nephos* 'cloud' +
L. *natare* 'to swim'.]

nethatch *(n.)*
an animal that is born in
captivity.

nomadromantic *(adj.)*
constantly travelling in
search of love.

nonconformula *(n.)*

the traditional routine of rebellion against society; unoriginal defiance.
[a blend of *nonconformism* + *formula*.]

nonemost *(adj.)*
the very least.

noodiefoodie *(n.)*
someone who eats naked.

nosetrim *(n.)*
a word formed by removing letters from the front of another word, such as umpkin or thologize.

nox-eyed *(adj.)*
able to see in the dark.
[from L. *nox* 'night' + *eyed*.]

nullaby *(n.)*
a minimalist lullaby that dispenses with words, sounds and other histrionics.
[a blend of L. *nullus* 'none' + *lullaby*.]

numerican *(n.)*
someone who is preoccupied with numbers.

O

obsense *(nm.)*
hidden meaning.
[from *ob-* + *sense*.]

oceantics *(pl. n.)*

outrageous underwater behaviour.
[a tiakler of *ocean* + *antics*.]

octopocketapus *(n.)*
an octopus that lives in a pocket.

odourtone *(n.)*
a smell combined with a sound.

olivelo *(n.)*
a fast fruit.
[a blend of *olive* + L. *velox* 'swift'.]

omegapsic *(adj., adv.)*
in reverse alphabetical order.
[from *omega* + *psi* + *-ic*.]

oodladatta *(nm., int.)*
too much information.
[a blend of *oodles* + *data*.]

oopsifluous *(adj.)*
providing many mistakes.
[from *oops* + L. *fluere* 'to flow' + *-ous*.]

opposium *(n.)*
a hall or room in which debates are held.

ork *(int.)*
an expression of surprise, disgust, etc.
[from It. *orco* 'monster'.]

otterbiography *(n.)*
a biography of an otter.

outfrox *(vt.)*
to trick someone into

taking their clothes off.
[a blend of *out* + *frock* +
outfox.]

outgrollop *(vt.)*
to grollop more quickly
than.

outh *(nm.)*
the state of being out.

outjarkle *(vt.)*
to jarkle more quickly than.
[from *out-* + Hp. *jarkle*.]

ovaltome *(n.)*
a novel, film, etc. with a
circular narrative, ending
where it began.

oversightly *(adj.)*
jarringly gorgeous.
[from *over-* + *sightly*.]

℘

pagefright *(nm.)*
nervousness about writing.

patchworthy *(adj.)*
eligible for repair.

peperiensive *(adj.)*
undead but not unidea'd.
[a blend of Hp. *peperious* +
pensive.]

peperious *(adj.)*
undead.
[from inf. *pep* 'energy' + L.
perire 'pass away' + *-ous*.]

pepstep *(n.)*
a living staircase.

[from inf. *pep* 'liveliness' +
step.]

picksocket *(n.)*
someone who illegally taps
into an electricity grid to
siphon power.

pigpie *(n.)*
a cross between a pigeon
and a magpie.
[a blend of *pigeon* +
magpie.]

piromancy *(nm.)*
divination of the value of
pi by creating circles of fire
with a fire staff or pois.
[a blend of *pi* + *rotate* +
pyromancy 'divination by
fire'.]

pixelanima *(n.)*
a living picture.
[from *pixel* + L. *anima*
'breath'.]

plasterguard *(n.)*
a tutelary statue.

ploughertower *(n.)*
an underground tower.

polkadice *(n.)*
a chance for a dance.

polydot *(n.)*
a multicellular organism.

poptometry *(nm.)*
eye-popping
measurements.
[a tiakler of *pop* +
optometry.]

praymate *(n.)*

someone who you worship
with.

pre-factual *(adj.)*
not yet true.

prepray *(vi.)*
to prudently seek divine
help for a bad situation in
advance.
[from *pre-* + *pray*.]

proxynonym *(n.)*
a word whose meaning is
close to that of another
word.
[a blend of *proximity* +
synonym.]

psammotroch *(n.)*
a wheel with spokes of
hourglasses intersecting at
their waists, the streams of
falling sand causing the
wheel to rotate perpetually.
[a blend of Gr. *psammos*
'sand' + Gr. *trokhos*
'wheel'.]

psittacoscintillaquill *(n.)*
a nocturnal parrot with
vivid plumage that glows
in the dark, usually with
rhythm and meaning.
[a blend of Gr. *psittakos*
'parrot' + L. *scintilla* 'spark'
+ *quill*.]

G

gabudgerilah *(n.)*

a cross between a galah
and a budgerigar.
[a blend of *galah* +
budgerigar.]

gaghaggler *(n.)*
a comedian's manager.

galawpus *(n.)*
someone who gazes
greedily.
[a blend of *galore* + *gawp*
+ *-us*.]

galecloud *(n.)*
a driven dreamer.

gazepticle *(n.)*
1. a tiny newspaper.
2. a news story presented
from a very narrow angle.
[from *gazette* + *zepto-* +
-cle.]

geckodile *(n.)*
a cross between a gecko
and a crocodile.

geologism *(n.)*
a word which is formed
underground.
[a blend of Gr. *ge* 'earth' +
neologism.]

getuppence *(n.)*
the amount of money worth
getting out of bed for.
[from *get* + *up* + *pence*.]

gherxite *(nm.)*
a vaguely green mineral
made of mashed,
carbonized cucumbers.
[from *gherkins* + *-ite*.]

gingoringe *(n.)*

a cross between a ginger
and an orange.
[a blend of *ginger* +
orange.]

glassmouse *(n.)*
a timid, honest person.

glissage *(nm.)*
the art of horses skating
and dancing on ice (with or
without riders).
[a blend of *glissade* +
dressage.]

glitchcraft *(nm.)*
the art of making mistakes.

gloomer *(n.)*
a glimmer of despair.
[a blend of *gloom* +
glimmer.]

glumdrop *(n.)*
a tear.

gnatcase *(n.)*
a tickbox with a screw
loose.

gnome de plume *(n.)*
a gnome with a feather in
his cap.
[from *gnome* + Fr. *de* 'of' +
plume.]

goblet *(n.)*
a young goblin.

godsmacked *(adj.)*
divinely punished.

golden reliever *(n.)*
a house-trained pet.

gooster *(n.)*
1. the offspring of a goose

and a rooster.
2. a larrikin.
[a blend of *goose* +
rooster.]

gorf *(vt./i.)*
to leapfrog backwards.
[a reversal of *frog*.]

grailblazer *(n.)*
someone who prefers hot
drinks to cold ones.

gravesore *(adj.)*
tired of being dead.

great-grasshopper *(n.)*
an insect ancestor.

griffery *(n.)*
a place where griffins are
kept or bred.

grimacious *(adj.)*
pulling faces.

grollop *(vi.)*
to walk like a caterpillar.
[a blend of *grub* + *lollop*.]

groundbound *(adj.)*
flightless.

grumbus *(n.)*
a mass of mushture floating
in the sky; a cloud of mud.
[a blend of *grubby* +
nimbus.]

gunflower *(nm.)*
popcorn.

gyrophyte *(n.)*
a rotating crop, such as a
turnip or a spinach.
[from *gyro-* + *-phyte*.]

R

ragglebloss *(n.)*
a feral bonsai plant.
[from Sc. obs. *raggle*
'straggling order' + Hp.
bloss.]

rainflake *(n.)*
a raindrop that has been
squashed, perhaps by a
fogmash or a heavy
atmosphere.

rambletash *(n.)*
a wandering moustache.
[from *ramble* + inf. *tash*
'moustache'.]

randaptivity *(nm.)*
cooperative chaos.
[a blend of *random* +
adaptivity.]

repellegance *(nm.)*
a compelling meld of
beauty and ugliness.
[a blend of *repel* +
elegance.]

resilienaire *(n.)*
a very hardy person.
[from *resilient* + -*aire*.]

reversalist *(n.)*
someone who prefers to do
things backwards.

riddlesome *(adj.)*
equipped with enigmas.

risket *(n.)*
a rice biscuit.
[a contraction of *rice
biscuit*.]

rollinghorse *(n.)*
a rocking horse whose
rockers extend 360° to
form wheels.

rosellaphant *(n.)*
a hybrid of a rosella and an
elephant.
[a blend of *rosella* +
elephant.]

rosellaphantine *(adj.)*
big and beautiful.
[from Hp. *rosellaphant* +
-*ine*.]

runebow *(n.)*
an alphabet.

ruxle *(vt.)*
to tamper with.
[a corruption of *rascal*.]

S

sagitagitate *(vt.)*
to annoy with arrows.
[a blend of L. *sagitta*
'arrow' + *agitate*.]

sandbasket *(n.)*
a basket made of sand.

saturacidophilate *(vt.)*
to drench in yogurt.
[a blend of *saturate* +
acidophilus.]

sausagophilous *(adj.)*
very fond of sausages.
[from *sausage* + -*philous*.]

scatterlax *(adj.)*
sprinkling offhandedly.

scramblegram *(n.)*
a mixed message.
[from *scramble* + *-gram*.]

scrambullion *(nm.)*
missing treasure.

scribbibble *(vt./i.)*
to drink words.
[a blend of *scribble* + obs. *bibble* 'to drink'.]

scrumptuous *(adj.)*
magnificent, rich and delicious.
[a blend of *scrumptious* + *sumptuous*.]

scruntletitle *(nm.)*
the right to be offended.
[a blend of *disgruntle* + *entitle*.]

seashine *(n.)*
a glow of the ocean caused by luminescent organisms.

semibiotic *(adj.)*
partially or reluctantly organic.
[from *semi-* + *biotic*.]

septizmal *(adj.)*
filthy and wretched.
[a blend of *septic* + *dismal*.]

serenadromous *(adj.)*
migrating upriver to croon, spoon and swoon.
[a blend of *serenade* + *anadromous*.]

seriffraph *(n.)*
a fallen angel.
[a blend of *seraph* + *riff-raff*.]

shankwrap *(vt.)*
to hug with the legs.

sharkspear *(n.)*
a small harpoon.

shatterpop *(vi.)*
to hatch from a test tube.

sheepshifter *(n.)*
a droving shepherd.

shuffalo *(n.)*
a breed of small, restless buffalo with very short legs.
[a blend of *shuffle* + *buffalo*.]

shushous *(adj.)*
calling for silence.

shyburn *(n.)*
a bold blush caused by social timidity.

sidegoing *(adj.)*
dodging slowly.

side-spoken *(adj.)*
tending to gossip.

silveracity *(nm.)*
bought truth.
[a tiakler of *silver* + *veracity*.]

simbian *(n.)*
a golden lion tamarin.
[a blend of *simba* 'lion' + *simian*.]

skirplicado *(nm.)*

the gentle art of creating decorative shapes by folding speeding tickets.
[from *skirr* 'to rush with a whirr' + L. *plicare* 'to fold' + *-ado*.]

skrooth *(vt./i.)*
to read.
[from L. *scrutari* 'examine' + *-th*.]

skuggle *(vt./i.)*
to juggle while skipping.
[a blend of *skip* + *juggle*.]

skurriboodle *(pl. n.)*
insects or other arthropods used as money.
[from *scurry* + inf. *boodle* 'money'.]

skweaver *(n.)*
a juggling ball with a long, ribbony tail.
[a blend of *sky* + *weaver*.]

skweavus *(n.)*
a juggler of skweavers.

skywinder *(n.)*
a living, flying, spiral staircase.

sloove *(n.)*
a section of a garment which encloses a leg.
[a variant of *sleeve*.]

sluglet *(n.)*
a young slug.

slybeguilage *(nm.)*
surreptitious seduction.

snaildust *(nm.)*

wet gunpowder.

snoize *(n.)*
a twisted sneeze.
[a variant of *sneeze*.]

snorbit *(n.)*
a full cycle of sleep stages.
[a blend of *snore* + *orbit*.]

snorbitorium *(n.)*
a sleep research laboratory.
[from Hp. *snorbit* + *-orium*.]

snorgle *(n.)*
an apparatus that allows you to snore underwater.
[a blend of *snore* + *gargle*.]

somebuddy *(pro.)*
an unspecified friend.
[a blend of *somebody* + *buddy*.]

sonatabud *(n.)*
a beautiful earlobe.

sparkthreads *(pl. n.)*
clothes made of material that is interwoven with electrical wiring to provide more warmth.

speaktrum *(n.)*
a person's speaking vocabulary.
[a blend of *speak* + *spectrum*.]

specifelicity *(nm.)*
elation from precision.
[a blend of *specificity* + *felicity*.]

specklesett *(n.)*

a decorated den.

spiceship *(n.)*
a commercial spacecraft
used to transport spice.
[a blend of *spice* +
spaceship.]

spinachuality *(nm.)*
the worship of vegetables.
[a blend of *spinach* +
spirituality.]

spinbeat *(n.)*
a whirlwind romance.

splinterment *(nm.)*
bitterness.

sprinklebang *(nm.)*
explosively hot spice.

stairport *(n.)*
a place where people got to
board a flying staircase.
[a tiakler of *stair* +
airport.]

staphenschlogg *(n.)*
a leg of dinosaur (as used
in cooking).
[from Ge. *stapfen* 'trudge' +
Ge. *Schlögel* 'leg'.]

startender *(n.)*
an assistant to a celebrity.

stepfarmer *(n.)*
someone who grows
pepsteps.

stokehouse *(n.)*
a theatre restaurant at
which the entertainment is
the cooking of the meals.
[a blend of *stoke*, in the

sense 'stimulate or incite' +
steakhouse.]

strawbridge *(n.)*
a tenuous connection.

stumblecrack *(n.)*
a joke that is just not
practical.

subvive *(vt./i.)*
to die, but only just.
[from *sub-* + L. *vivere* 'to
live'.]

suduration *(n.)*
the time it takes to have a
bath.
[an elboword of *sud* +
duration.]

sureshift *(n.)*
a smooth transition.

swa-ching *(n.)*
a dance that combines cha-
cha with swing.
[a blend of *swing* + *cha-
cha*.]

swade *(vi.)*
to dance slowly in shallow
water.
[a blend of *sway* + *wade*.]

swavoureet *(adj.)*
both sweet and savoury.
[a blend of *sweet* +
savoury.]

swayline *(n.)*
the edge of conviction.

sybaranklement *(nm.)*
self-indulgent indignation.
[from *sybaritic* + *rankle* +

-*ment*.]

sylvarhize *(n.)*
a root of a forest.
[a blend of L. *silva* 'wood'
+ Gr. *rhiza* 'root'.]

T

taggenite *(n.)*
a spur or goad.
[a variant of *antagonize*.]

tailstone *(n.)*
an inscribed stone that
marks the location of
someone's birth.

tentboat *(n.)*
a small houseboat.

tenterment *(n.)*
a stretchy imagination.
[a blend of L. *tendere* 'to
stretch' + L. *mens* 'mind'.]

terfluppify *(vt.)*
1. to rearrange beyond all
recognition.
2. to faze.
[from *ter-* + Hp. *flupple* +
-*fy*.]

tergrollopous *(adj.)*
promenading majestically.
[from *ter-* + Hp. *grollop* +
-*ous*.]

tetherfrayed *(adj.)*
hopeful.

theotropism *(n.)*
the tendency of certain

plants to turn towards God.
[from *theo-* + *tropism*.]

thestervex *(n.)*
a whirlpool of darkness.
[a blend of obs. *thester*
'darkness' + *vortex*.]

thologize *(vt.)*
to edit excessively.
[a nosetrim of
mythologize.]

thorcavought *(n.)*
a dancing idea.
[a blend of *thought* +
cavort.]

thoroughbread *(nm.)*
wholemeal bread.

thoughtoise *(n.)*
a ponderous, pondering
reptile with slow, heavy
thoughts.
[a blend of *thought* +
tortoise.]

thranket *(n.)*
a part of a machine whose
only function is to make
people wonder what its
function is.
[derivation unknown.]

threadlocks *(pl. n.)*
very thin hair.

thry- *(prefix)*
1. a variant of tri-; three.
2. used as an intensifier.
[from *three*.]

thryfare *(n.)*
a wonderful experience.

[from thry- + *fare*.]

thudbust *(n.)*
an explosion caused by an impact.

thunket *(n.)*
a large parcel.
[a blend of inf. *thunk* 'thud' + *packet*.]

thwarble *(vt./i.)*
to sing underwater.
[a variant of *warble*.]

thwink *(vt./i.)*
to think twice.
[a blend of *think* + *twice*.]

tiakler *(n.)*
a blend word in which the second word begins with the last two or more letters of the first word, such as silveracity from silver and veracity.
[derivation unknown.]

tickbox *(n.)*
a small cage in which to accommodate a pet insect.

ticryptochronize *(vt.)*
to hide something in another time.
[a blend of *tick-tock* + *crypto-* + *chrono-* + *-ize*.]

tidalstride *(n.)*
a clog hewn from driftwood.

tingalingualinger *(vi.)*
to hesitate on the tip of your lover's tongue.
[a blend of *tingle* + L.

lingua 'tongue' + *linger*.]

tivatorium *(n.)*
a museum of illusions.
[from *captivate* + *-orium*.]

todaily *(adj., adv.)*
as soon and often as possible.

tofkea *(nm.)*
a mixture of tea and coffee.
[a blend of *tea* + *coffee*.]

tofkealapper *(n.)*
someone who can't decide what to choose, so they choose everything.
[from Hp. *tofkea* + *lapper*.]

toleather *(adv., adj.)*
on horseback.

tomaletous *(adj.)*
containing tomato and lettuce.
[a blend of *tomato* + *lettuce* + *-ous*.]

toofaa *(adj.)*
excessive.

toothdresser *(n.)*
a cosmetic dentist.

tortfrort *(adj.)*
crawling with twists.
[a blend of L. *tortus* 'twisted' + *fraught*.]

treadmire *(n.)*
a jumble of footprints.

trebletherent *(adj.)*
prattling in a high-pitched voice.
[a blend of *treble* + *blether*

'blather' + -*ent*.]

tresspassaway *(vi.)*
to illegally gain access to an afterworld.
[a tiakler of *trespass* + *pass away*.]

tricador *(n.)*
an accomplished and respected trickster.
[a blend of *trick* + *picador*.]

trigonogamy *(nm.)*
the social science of love triangles.
[from *trigonometry* + -*gamy*.]

trikinilby *(n.)*
a three-piece bathing costume consisting of a bikini and a trilby.
[a blend of *trilby* + *bikini*.]

tubecube *(n.)*
a bale of bucatini.

tuitex *(nm.)*
the fabric of space-time.
[derivation uncertain; probably a blend of *perpetuity* + *textile*.]

tumbledrum *(n.)*
a performer who does acrobatics while playing a drum.

turby *(n.)*
a washing machine.
[from L. *turbo* 'whirl' + -*y*.]

twelvence *(nm.)*
abundance.

[from *twelve* + -*ence*.]

twinklepop *(n.)*
a cute, little supernova.

twistep *(n.)*
a living, supple, winding staircase that is able to contort itself into many different shapes.
[a tiakler of *twist* + *step*.]

U

umbatumba *(n.)*
an avalanche of shadows.
[a blend of L. *umbra* 'shadow' + *tumble*.]

umbelliver *(n.)*
an irreligious plant.
[a blend of *umbellifer* + *unbeliever*.]

umbricorn *(n.)*
a species of horse with an umbrella protruding from its forehead.
[a blend of *umbrella* + *unicorn*.]

umpkin *(n.)*
a scalped pumpkin.
[a nosetrim of *pumpkin*.]

unamuse *(vt.)*
to depress someone by telling them a joke backwards.

underbuzz *(nm.)*
concealed or repressed excitement.

unfetterccini *(nm.)*
free-range pasta.
[a blend of *unfettered* +
fettuccini.]

unheedhankerage *(nm.)*
a desire to be ignored.

upsitting *(adj.)*
sitting up straight.

upspark *(n.)*
a great idea you have just
as you're waking up.

upstem *(adv., adj.)*
towards or nearer to the
roots.

uptrain *(adv.)*
towards the back of a train.
[from *up-* + *train*.]

V

vacubore *(n.)*
a tool that drills holes by
suction.
[a blend of *vacuum* +
bore.]

vagulatrous *(adj.)*
tending to wander about
when praying.
[from L. *vagus* 'wandering'
-latry + *-ous*.]

vainaim *(nm.)*
purpose without meaning.

velodrama *(n.)*
an exciting play with fast-
moving action.

[a blend of L. *velox* 'swift'
+ *drama*.]

vlankernapes *(n.)*
an electric monkey.
[a blend of dialect *vlanker*
'spark of fire' + *jackanapes*
'tame ape'.]

voidcast *(adj.)*
defined by emptiness.

volagrad *(n.)*
a living, flying staircase.
[a blend of L. *volare* 'to fly'
+ L. *gradus* 'step'.]

volgolfano *(nm.)*
a sport in which players
attempt to hit a large
hailstone into an active
volcano to put it out.
[a blend of *volcano* + *golf*.]

W

wanderponder *(vt./i.)*
to think by walking.

wanderpondersome *(adj.)*
apt to wanderponder.

warpertortuosity *(n.)*
a living water slide that
wriggles and squirms.
[a blend of *warp* + *water* +
tortuosity.]

watchful *(n.)*
the amount of time that a
watch can carry.

watermobile *(n.)*

a boat.

waybeforce *(nm.)*
the might of antiquity.
[a blend of *way* + *before* +
force.]

weavegrove *(n.)*
a forest of vines.

weavil *(n.)*
a beetle that uses its sturdy
rostrum to recount
convoluted stories.
[a blend of *weave* +
weevil.]

wellago *(adv., adj.)*
in or into the distant past.
[from *well* + *ago*.]

whalewade *(vi.)*
to dabble deeply.

whimsday *(n.)*
a day on which routines are
ceremoniously broken.

wicknix *(adj.)*
having run out of candles.
[from *wick* + inf. *nix*
'nothing'.]

wingbrow *(n.)*
a visionary thinker.

wistefoist *(n.)*
an unwelcome desire.
[a blend of *wistful* + *foist*.]

witherbrush *(n.)*
a painter who's past his
primer.

woehide *(n.)*
a place where it is safe to
be sad.

wolfare *(nm.)*
the well-being of wolves.
[a blend of *wolf* + *welfare*.]

woofle *(n.)*
a swavoureet cross
between a hot dog and a
waffle.
[a blend of *woof* + *waffle*.]

wormalade *(n.)*
a jam made from bitter
oranges and even bitterer
worms.
[a blend of *worm* +
marmalade.]

worthforth *(nm.)*
the power of dignity.

wovenwing *(nm.)*
knitted plumage.

wrigglebreak *(n.)*
a contortionist who is also
an escapologist.

wriggular *(adj.)*
nervous.
[from *wriggle* + *-ular*.]

wundle *(n.)*
a book.
[a blend of *word* + *bundle*.]

y

yaggle *(n.)*
one of those strings found
under the skin of a banana.
[a blend of *yellow* +
straggle.]

yaulk *(n.)*
the yolk of an auk's egg.
[a blend of *yolk* + *auk*.]

yearlier *(adv.)*
more yearly.

yonderling *(n.)*
a foreigner.
[from *yonder* + *-ling*.]

yondoon *(n.)*
tomorrow.
[a blend of *yonder* + *noon*.]

youthe *(vi.)*
to grow younger.

yurtyacht *(n.)*
a houseboat in the form of a circular, cruisy tent with luxurious felt sails.

intense feeling expressed slightly.
[a variant of *zeal*.]

zippermint *(n.)*
a clothes factory.

zoombroom *(n.)*
a tool used for gathering momentum.

zooqueue *(n.)*
a long line of different animals waiting to board a train, ark, etc.

zumblebudge *(n.)*
a propulsive snore.
[a blend of Sp. *zumbar* 'to hum' + *rumble* + *budge*.]

Z

zacket *(n.)*
a ruler (for measuring).
[a variant of *exact*.]

zafferona *(n.)*
1. a kite.
2. an ideal.
[a blend of Ar. *zarafa* 'giraffe' + L. *corona* 'crown'.]

zedify *(vt.)*
to deem least important.

zesper *(n.)*
a rousing prayer.
[a blend of *zest* + *vespers*.]

zill *(nm.)*

The End.

About the Author

As a baby, David spoke his first word at only three weeks, but unfortunately it was unintelligible. Even though he clearly repeated "unintelligible" several times, he couldn't seem to get the point across, so he gave up and mumbled "distinctly" instead.

As a child, he started making up silly words, but it was only after much practice that they became severely silly.

As an adult, he was drawn deeper and deeper into the mystery of linguistics, and eventually he found, at its core, the ineffable. He was so dumbstruck that he dropped all his decibels.

www.hoptanglish.com

www.ingramcontent.com/pod-product-compliance
Lightning Source LLC
Chambersburg PA
CBHW030310030426
42337CB00012B/663